Who Works Here?

Construction Site

by Lola M. Schaefer

Heinemann Library
Chicago, Illinois

©2000 Reed Educational & Professional Publishing
Published by Heinemann Library,
an imprint of Reed Educational & Professional Publishing,
100 N. LaSalle, Suite 1010
Chicago, IL 60602
Customer Service 888-454-2279

Printed in Hong Kong
Designed by Made in Chicago Design Associates

04 03 02 01 00
10 9 8 7 6 5 4 3 2 1

Library of Congress Cataloging-in-Publication Data

Schaefer, Lola M., 1950
     Construction site / Lola Schaefer.
       p. cm. – (Who works here?)
     Includes bibliographical references and index.
     Summary: An introduction to the people who work at a construction
site, including salespeople, site excavator, contractor, framer,
painter, plumber, and electrician.
     ISBN 1-57572-516-9 (library binding)
     1. Building Juvenile literature. 2. Construction workers Juvenile
literature.   [1. Construction workers. 2. Building.
3. Occupations.]   I. Title. II. Series.
     TH149.S33   2000
     690—dc21   99-40773
                                                         CIP

Acknowledgments
All photographs by Phil Martin.

Special thanks to Pete Balistreri and all the workers at William Ryan Homes in Huntley, Illinois, and to workers everywhere who take pride in what they do.

Every effort has been made to contact copyright holders of any material reproduced in this book. Any omissions will be rectified in subsequent printings if notice is given to the publisher.

Some words are shown in bold, **like this.**
You can find out what they mean by looking in the glossary.

Contents

What Is a Construction Site?

A construction site is a busy place where new buildings are being built. A housing development begins when a homebuilder buys land and plans a neighborhood. Salespeople sell **lots** and houses to be built. The homebuilder hires **contractors** to build the houses.

Many contractors work together to build strong, safe houses. Construction begins with digging a hole for the **foundation.** It ends with **landscaping** a yard around the house. People always need new homes. Look around—there might be a construction site near you.

This construction site is in Huntley, Illinois. The map shows all of the places where the people in this book are working. Many construction sites in the United States look like this.

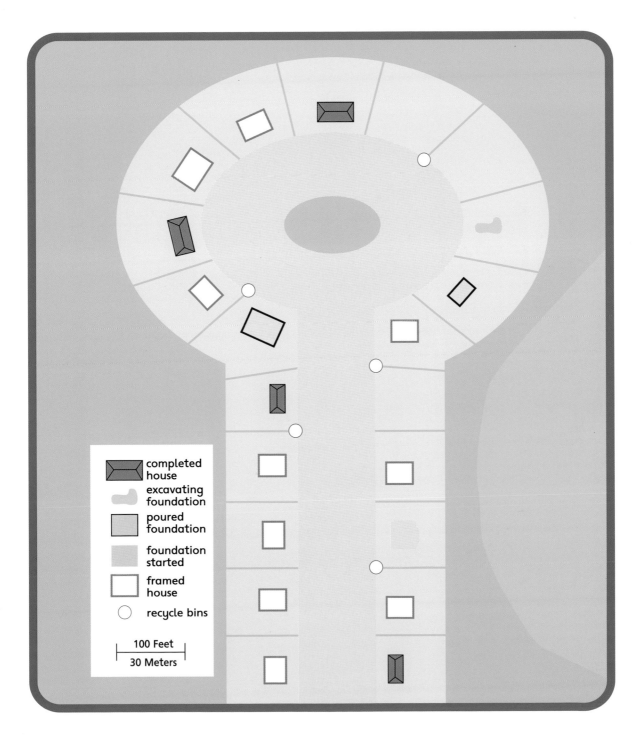

completed house

excavating foundation

poured foundation

foundation started

framed house

○ recycle bins

100 Feet
30 Meters

Salesperson

A salesperson for a homebuilder shows plans to future home buyers. The salesperson takes the home buyers through **model** houses. If a home buyer wants to buy a **lot** and house, the salesperson prepares a **contract** for the buyer to sign.

Avery (on the left) is a salesperson. He must be able to answer questions about the house plans and the development.

Avery offers a contract to a home buyer.

A good salesperson learns by working with homebuilders. The salesperson should know all the features that a house can have and how much they cost. This way, the salesperson can help home buyers find the best house to meet their needs.

Superintendent

The superintendent of this development is Wayne (on the right). Here he talks with a contractor about changes to a house plan.

The superintendent of a construction site is in charge of keeping all the **contractors** working on schedule. The superintendent visits the houses as they are built. The most important part of the superintendent's job is keeping everything going well between homeowners and contractors.

Wayne, like many superintendents, worked in the **building trades** for many years before he became superintendent. He knows every job in the construction business. Superintendents must understand how homes are built. Working outdoors and meeting new people are two things Wayne likes about his job.

Wayne must talk and listen closely to the homeowners. Here he is talking with a homeowner about new sidewalks.

Site Excavator

Ed is a site excavator at this development. He drives an earth-moving machine called an excavator. Here he lowers the bucket to dig out the dirt.

The site excavator is the person who digs the hole for the **foundation** of a house. Later, the excavator pushes dirt back around the concrete foundation. At the end of the job, the excavator smooths the ground around the house.

Ed, like many excavators, received his training on the job. Excavators learn how to use big and small earth-moving machines safely. Site excavators dig, lift, carry, and dump dirt or stone. They dig driveways and sidewalks and later carry stone to those forms.

Ed uses the levers inside the cab to move the excavator.

Using a Laser Planer and Level

The site excavator places the laser planer on top of a tripod.

When excavators dig a **foundation,** they use a laser planer. The planer sends out a **laser beam.** The beam moves back and forth across the construction site at one height. Ed uses this as a guide to **program** his laser **level.** The planer helps the excavator dig the foundation to the correct depth and makes sure the foundation is level.

The laser level sits on the arm of the excavator. Ed programs the computer inside the level. The laser beam from the planer scans the level. When Ed is in the excavator cab, he can read the level.

The red light in the middle signals the excavator to dig at that depth.

Concrete Contractors

Concrete **contractors** build **foundations** with concrete. Using shovels, they dig **footings** around the foundation hole. Then they place boards down to make a form. The cement truck comes and pours wet concrete into the footings.

Scott and Tony are concrete contractors. Here they are getting ready to spread the concrete in the forms.

Concrete contractors work near large machines. They protect their feet by wearing heavy work boots. They protect their hands with thick gloves. When work is going on above them, they wear hard hats to protect their heads. Safety is very important to these workers.

This concrete contractor uses a hand tool to smooth a basement wall.

Framer

Framers build the outside walls of a house with boards. They also make the frame for the roof. Framers nail large sheets of wood to the frame to form the walls. Near the end of the job, they nail the floorboards in place.

Framers use nail guns to construct the frame. Nail guns shoot nails quickly and securely into wood.

Framers need to measure and cut each board carefully. Framers use **levels** to make sure each wall is standing straight. It takes about two days for a crew to frame a house. Then, the other **contractors** begin work on the inside.

Framers have completed most of this first floor.

Heating and Air-conditioning Contractor

Ken is a heating and air-conditioning contractor. Here, he is installing a flexible hose for a bathroom fan.

A heating and air-conditioning **contractor** puts together and **installs** the **ducts** that run from the furnace. The contractor also installs pipes and vents for the clothes dryer and the kitchen and bathroom fans. The contractor carefully cuts and measures **sheet metal** to make the vents and ducts.

It usually takes about three years for a heating and air-conditioning contractor to learn the job well. Ken, like many other contractors, studied as he worked with other heating and air-conditioning contractors. During this time, he learned how to bend metal pieces to fit them together.

Ken tapes the seam in a pipe to make it stronger and safer.

Plumber

Leon is a plumber at this construction site.
Here he cuts a drain pipe in the basement.

The plumbers at a construction site **install** pipes for the water and natural gas coming in and going out of a house. Plumbers also install drains. A plumber spends much of the day cutting pipe and attaching **fittings**.

Many plumbers, like Leon, spent four years learning the trade. Plumbers learn to be careful when **soldering** pipes together. First, they clean the pipes on the ends. Then, wearing safety glasses, the plumber uses a torch to melt the solder onto the pipes. The solder holds the pipes together.

Leon solders two water pipes.

Electrician

Bill, an electrician at the construction site, drills a hole to the second floor.

An electrician **installs** electrical wire in houses. Some wire needs to be placed in plastic or metal tubes for safety. To wire a house, the electrician drills holes in the frame and puts the tubes through the holes. Then, the electrician runs the electrical wire throughout the house.

Bill uses a power screwdriver to install a switch.

Like many electricians, Bill had five years of training and schooling to become an electrician. Electricians need to know the best and safest way to install electrical boxes for outlets. They must know how to install and wire switches for lights and fans. Homeowners are happy that trained electricians wire their homes safely.

Drywall Contractor

Carlos, the drywall contractor, spreads plaster on the ceiling.

A drywall **contractor installs** drywall on the inside of the house frame. Drywall is a sheet of plasterboard. After all the drywall is up, the drywall contractor spreads wet plaster on the **seams.** The contractor must wear stilts to reach the high places.

After plastering between the seams, the drywall contractor puts tape on the seams. Then, the seams are plastered again. The last step is sanding until the wall is smooth for paint or wallpaper. It takes several years to learn how to install and prepare drywall correctly. Drywall contractors learn all the steps in this **building trade**.

Carlos uses a pole to sand the seams so that the paint will be smooth.

Painter

Tom is one of the painters working at the construction site. Here he uses a roller to paint a large wall.

Painters prepare and paint the inside walls and woodwork in a house. First, the painters patch, sand, and put a **finish** on the woodwork. Then, they cover the woodwork so they don't spill paint on it. Finally, the painters can paint the walls the color the homeowner has chosen.

Some painters, such as Tom, went to a trade school for three years. There, they learned the proper way to prepare wood and drywall for finishes. Painters learn how to protect themselves from dust and fumes by wearing a **respirator** correctly.

A respirator keeps the sanding dust and painting fumes out of the painter's lungs.

Cardboard Baler Driver

When much of the construction is complete, a cardboard baler truck driver visits the construction site. This person stops at recycle bins and takes out the cardboard boxes. The driver flattens each box and puts it into a baler on the back of the truck. The baler presses the cardboard and places it into a **bale**.

Ben is a cardboard baler truck driver. Here he feeds cardboard into the baler.

The cardboard baler driver stops
the truck next to a recycle bin.

Each morning, the driver's company gives him or her a
route. The driver visits many sites and collects enough
cardboard every day to make two bales. One bale weighs
two thousand pounds (nine hundred kilograms). The bales
are later recycled into new cardboard products.

Glossary

bale large bundle of things tied tightly together

building trade skilled work with the hands or machines that is used in constructing buildings

contract legal agreement between people or companies stating the price and terms by which work or a product will be sold

contractor person who supplies materials or performs work for a price

duct tube that carries air or liquid from one place to another

finish coating on the surface of metal, wood, or drywall

fitting small metal or plastic part that connects things like pipes or drains

footing bottom part of a foundation

foundation solid base on which a building is built, usually made of concrete

install to put something in place for service or use

landscaping changing and improving the looks of an area of land

laser beam very narrow, powerful beam of light made by a laser

level tool used to find a perfectly flat line or surface

lot small area of land on which a house can be built

model display house that shows the style and design of others

program to give information and instructions to a computer to make it work in a certain way

respirator masklike device worn over the nose and mouth that prevents the person from breathing harmful materials

route list of places to stop

seam line where the edges of two pieces of material join

sheet metal thin pieces of aluminum or steel that can be shaped into ducts or pipes

solder to join pieces of metal with a hot, liquid metal that hardens as it cools

More Books to Read

Deedrick, Tami. *Construction Workers.* Mankato, Minn.: Bridgestone Books, 1998.

Eick, Jean. *Excavators.* Edina, Minn.: ABDO & Daughters, 1997.

Gibbons, Gail. *How a House Is Built.* New York: Holiday House, 1990.

Jackson, Thomas Campbell. *Hammers, Nails, Planks, and Paint: How a House Is Built.* New York: Cartwheel Books, 1994.

Schomp, Virginia. *If You Were a Construction Worker.* New York: Benchmark Books, 1998.

Index